Tropical Landscape
with Ten Hummingbirds

Poems by

GREG RAPPLEYE

DOS MADRES

2018

DOS MADRES PRESS INC.

P.O.Box 294, Loveland, Ohio 45140

www.dosmadres.com   editor@dosmadres.com

Dos Madres is dedicated to the belief that the small press is essential to the vitality of contemporary literature as a carrier of the new voice, as well as the older, sometimes forgotten voices of the past. And in an ever more virtual world, to the creation of fine books pleasing to the eye and hand.

Dos Madres is named in honor of Vera Murphy and Libbie Hughes, the "Dos Madres" whose contributions have made this press possible.

Dos Madres Press, Inc. is an Ohio Not For Profit Corporation and a 501 (c) (3) qualified public charity. Contributions are tax deductible.

Executive Editor: Robert J. Murphy

Illustration & Book Design: Elizabeth H. Murphy
www.illusionstudios.net
Cover: Detail of *Orchid and Hummingbird* (1885)
by Martin Johnson Heade

Typeset in Adobe Garamond Pro & Footlight MT
ISBN 978-1-948017-25-1
Library of Congress Control Number: 2018955398

First Edition

ACKNOWLEDGEMENTS

My thanks to the editors of the following magazines and journals in which some of these poems originally appeared, sometimes in slightly different forms:

"Letter to Harriet Beecher Stowe," "On Martin Johnson Heade's *Approaching Thunderstorm* (1859)," "Studies for *The Blue Morpho* (1864)," and "Tarantula" appeared in *Arts & Letters*, and won the *Arts & Letters* Prize in Poetry

"Orpheus Gathering the Trees," appeared in *Bellingham Review*, and in *Making Poems: Forty Poems with Commentary by the Poets* edited by Todd Davis and Erin Murphy (SUNY Press, 2010)

Excerpt from an Unsent Letter to Mrs. Laura Webb, Regarding *Ruby Throat of North America* (1865)," "*Thorntails, Brazil* (1863-1864)," "Orpheus Considers His Approach to Cerberus," "Orpheus, Adrift," "Orpheus the Prophet," and "*Two Hummingbirds with their Young* (1864)" appeared in the *Legal Studies Forum*

"*Flying Down to Rio* (1933)," "*Orfeu Negro* (1959)," and "Donald Duck in Brazil" appeared in *Blue Fifth Review*

Insomnia, with Sappho Comet" appeared in *The Naugatuck River Review*

"*It's All True* (1942)" appeared in *The Magic Lantern Review*

"Letter to Frederic Edwin Church at Olana," and "Letter to Bridget Campbell in Tobago," appeared in *Poemeleon*

"Orpheus Speaks," "The Response of Eurydice," and "By Oil Lamp, the Hummingbird Artist Decants a Glass of Madeira and Contemplates *Hooded Visorbearer*," appeared in POEM

"Robert Mitchum Returns to the Blue Haven Hotel" appeared in *The Quotable*

"A Study of Rosa Gonzales," and "Notes of Capitao Eduardo Gonzales in Preparation for a Report to His Excellency Baron de Temandere, First Admiral and Commander of the Brazilian Imperial Navy, Regarding the Activities of the American Painter, Martin Johnson Heade" appeared in *Shenandoah*

"*Sun Gems* (ca. 1864-1865)" and "The Apprentice Lithographer's Story" appeared in *The Valparaiso Poetry Review*

"The Origami Hummingbirds" appeared in *Bosque*

"The Hummingbird Artist Dreams of the Ladder of Heaven" will appear in *Footnote: A Literary Journal of History* and is currently a semi-finalist for the 2019 Charter Oak Award for Historical Writing

My great thanks to fellow poets Jane Harrington Bach and Jack Ridl for their patience and good counsel as we worked through this manuscript. Special thanks to Jeff Cunningham for his repeated encouragement. Thanks also to my students and colleagues at Hope College. I owe so much to the vision, skill and faith of Robert J. Murphy and Elizabeth H. Murphy at Dos Madres Press. Forever, thank-you. As always, my greatest debt is owed to Marcia Kennedy Rappleye, *stealing kisses of water, of flowers, of air.*

For Florence Arenz
(1928-2010)

TABLE OF CONTENTS

INTRODUCTION

On September 2, 1863, in the depths of the Civil War, the American painter Martin Johnson Heade sailed for Brazil, to paint the hummingbirds of that extravagantly jungled country, with an ultimate goal of having his paintings printed in Europe and bound in elegant limited editions, and to thereby secure his fame and fortune. Under the hypnotic spell of that mysterious land, its people, and its hummingbirds, Heade made his paintings too complex; so wildly excessive in colors, in drama, in landscape and flora, that no press of that day could fully replicate what Heade intended.

Greg Rappleye's luminous fourth full-length volume of poetry invites the reader to join Heade on his artistic quest, and in a series of more than forty exquisitely realized poems, tells the story of Heade's passionate work during his sojourn in Brazil, of his thwarted desires and inevitable tragic failure in London, and of an ultimate triumph of a uniquely American kind, for the original hummingbird paintings of Martin Johnson Heade and the work his "failed" journey to Brazil inspired, are now regarded as treasures of 19th Century American art.

Heade's story, imagined through the wit, elegance, and sharp consciousness of Rappleye's poems, flavored with poignant, funny, wonderfully wrought work starring such unlikely characters as Fred Astaire, Donald Duck, Rita Hayworth, Orpheus, Jack Lemon and Robert Mitchum, reveal Greg Rappleye to be what many have long suspected in the years since his second collection *A Path Between Houses,* won the prestigious Brittingham Prize in 2000—that he is one of America's most promising and versatile poets, beginning here to approach the very height of his powers.

The Boston Transcript, which had commented favorably on [Martin Johnson] Heade's work regularly since 1858, reported on August 12, 1863, that "M. J. Heade, Esq., the artist so well known for his landscapes...is about to visit Brazil, to paint those winged jewels, the hummingbirds, in all their varieties of life as found beneath the tropics." The article added that the painter, aiming to fulfill "the dream of his boyhood," was planning "to prepare in London or Paris a large and elegant album on these wonderful little creatures, got up in the highest style of art." Heade himself takes up the story next, in his invaluable Brazil-London Journal. He begins, "The steamer Golden City left N.Y. Sept 2nd 1863; arrived Rio de Janeiro on Sunday night September 20th—making passage in less than 19 days."

—THEODORE STEBBINS, JR.
The Life and Work of Martin Johnson Heade:
A Critical Analysis and Catalogue Raisonné (2000),
"Painter of the Tropics," p. 61

True singing is a different breath, about nothing. A gust inside a god, a wind.

—RAINER MARIA RILKE
The Sonnets to Orpheus, I, 3

"A Vast Rosewood Aviary Containing Approximately 150 Live Hummingbirds with Fresh Specimens Arriving…"

-Frank M. Chapman, *Ornithology at the World's Fair,*
The Auk: Journal of the American Ornithologist's Union, June, 1893

Mrs. Rosa Gonzales Anderson at the Pavilion of Brazil,
The World's Columbian Exposition, Chicago, July 27, 1893

Beyond the mullioned glass, humming
near a sculpted pond—Golden Throats,
Woodstars, Streamertails—others

she no longer knows—vermillion, green.
The hummingbirds scatter, they dab
at gardenias and re-form—

trellised through vines and hibiscus—
so-la-ti—tiny songs always in flux—
breve and semi-breve, quaver and minim.

A tilt of sun from an open skylight
angles across the room. Greenery in clay pots
and the purple fruit of the tortoise tree.

What she feels must pass for yearning—
a back-screen of far-off hills, her rainy country
so distant. It is hard not to speak

in her native tongue—*colibris, beija flor.*
The hummingbirds rise and fall—
stealing kisses of water, of flowers, of air.

Letter to Harriet Beecher Stowe

From the American Painter Martin Johnson Heade
in Rio de Janeiro, October 24, 1863

Now in his heart, Ahab had some glimpse of this,
namely: all my means are sane, my motive and my
object mad.
—Herman Melville, *Moby Dick*
or The Great Whale (1851), Chapter XLI

Your letter arrived two days past, aboard
the twelve-gun *Sabine,* under the command
of Lieutenant Robert Adams, late of Hartford.
My guide and companion, Eduardo Gonzales,
Captain of the Brazilian Imperial Navy,
asked that I go with him to the docks
to greet the visiting warship.
Brazil, of course, remains neutral
in the great American conflict,
though it is difficult to assay the feelings
of the people, who follow the dispatches
with great and voluble interest. There is
a fair sized American community here,
with both Union and rebel sympathies.
Spies and rumors of saboteurs abound;
the port is open to provisioning by both sides.
To wander the docks before dawn—
weaving through dark bundles and nameless casks—
is to know considerable risk. One hears American voices
urging the lethargic porters—*Work faster! Faster!*
Mais rapidamente! The masters of these ships—
Southern, Northern, or mysteriously non-allied—
hope to slip their lines and vanish
on the next outbound tide. My cause is mundane.

My goal—to paint the hummingbirds of this
jungled land, and have those paintings
lithographed on the great presses of London,
where they might be subscribed-to
in elegant limited editions,
in the manner of Audubon and Gould,
and thereby secure, if not my fortune,
perhaps a lasting name. As title for this volume
I settle upon *Gems of Brazil*, for that is
what these hummers are. One thinks of jewels
when watching them sip nectar
or in buzzy, ecstatic flight—
of honey rich ambers, of bright sapphires,
of rubies and purple amethysts, bodies fired
by the dappled light of this riotously fecund land,
where every swale is wreathed with passion
flowers, with gardenias and sweet orchids.
One must recall that admonition
written in Proverbs, echoed in the Book of Job—
The price of wisdom is above rubies, and pray
my extravagant joy in this work
does not bring a tragic end.

Saddened to learn of your son's wound
at Gettysburg, I pray for his health. Tales
of the valiant hour of the Massachusetts artillery
before Pickett's charge at that fateful ridge,
reached us in a packet of dailies
which sailed aboard *The Cartagena*.
The description of the rebel barrage
on the day of Captain Stowe's head injury—

"Splintered shells and fiendish wailings,
like the predatory howls
of demons in search of their prey,"
astonished the Americans here; the Union
owes a great debt to Captain Stowe.
My best to Frederick. Remember me to all.

As you know, Brazil still suffers the curse of slavery.
Through the intercession of the Reverend Fletcher
and the American consul, the Honorable James Monroe,
I was introduced to Emperor Dom Pedro II.
Upon learning that you were a friend, he asked
if I might secure on his account
a copy of your great and famous book.
If you could send one, inscribed,
through American diplomatic channels, I will assure
its delivery to His Imperial Majesty,
in the hope your work will bring as much
to this benighted land as it has to our United States.
Until that day, I remain,
your devoted servant, et cetera.

On Martin Johnson Heade's
Approaching Thunderstorm (1859)

"This is a beautiful country."
-John Brown, remark as he rode to the gallows,
seated on his coffin (December 2, 1859)

The sky spread with charcoal clouds.
Beneath, a dove-gray meant as distant rain, falling
across darker hills, beyond a lacquer-black bay.
Dead center, a white-sailed catboat has either made the point
of the inner harbor, and will be home as the sky opens,
or the catboat has not made the point
and must come about again,
meaning the sailors will not be safely home.
How the odd light reaches—the creamy bloom of the sail,
a catboat moving too serenely—the sun, startling the far-left point,
the one the sailors must make, then circling to fire the grass
of the closer point.

                    Do not fear for the man in the rowboat,
who has made his turn and pulls for the green shore.
Do not fear for the man in the straw hat, red shirt,
tan vest—seated in the foreground, smoking a pipe.
No fear, either, for his dog—a yellow lab, I'd say—
perhaps the first of this breed in American art.
But what of the man you can barely see? He is no more
than a cross of rose madder and flesh, standing
at the sole of the catboat,
facing the mouth of the inner harbor,
the seated man and his ardent yellow lab.
In the foreground, draping a rock, the shroud of a larger sail
the captain did not take when he left. Everywhere—

the water is luminously black, the sea, so eerily calm.
The catboat is not yet up on its heel, the men have not begun
to work for the point. It seems they never will.

Tarantula

The American painter Martin Johnson Heade in Brazil,
near the mountain resort of Petropolis, November 2, 1863

Emerald green, spring green, viridian.
Thalo green, cadmium green, and behind this,
along the face of the forty foot cliff, sea-green lichens,
moss, a depth of woody, twisting vines—
black, burnt orange, purplish browns—
riotously twined with orchids and flowers
of great variety: passion flowers, gardenias,
flowers sipping moisture from air; their florid colors—
pinks, lavenders, oranges, so many reds—
that color most favored, it would seem, by all
hummingbirds. And the mysteries
of the extravagant leaves
that shade the face of the escarpment.
I had gone early that morning, several miles south
of the city, along the *Estrada Real*
with Capitao Gonzales, his lovely sister Rosa,
her several Negro servants.
My plan—to sketch where I had seen
so many hummers on the carriage ride from Rio.

I was drawing trumpet flowers,
behind me, Rosa and her servants, arranging tea
across a rosewood table. The hummingbirds
were Brazilian Rubies—six to eight males—
iridescent green with pinkish-red throats—
shining, flaming—throats like hungry mouths.
The females—there were many—were
also weaving, buzzing, feeding—the birds,
arrayed like hovered angels.

I found myself in a reverie—quick,
though not conscious of my haste,
my sketch pad in-hand or resting atop
my lap desk; a faint, busy thrum
in the pollen thick air—a stirring,
when a hummingbird, seemingly oblivious,
passed by my head.

                    Suddenly, from where
the leaves opened to the deepest dark, a tarantula—
large, hairy, black, no—gray, with fur tips
nearly salmon-colored, big as my fist—
here are my sketches, drawn from a flash of memory—
jumped from behind a leaf
and took a hummer in midair!
They seemed to hang, shimmering
in the dappled light—a ball
of demonic legs, salmon-tinted fur,
and the red-and-green of the doomed bird,
the near invisible flutter of wings, a pause
and then the fall—plummeting
into a tangle of darkness and vines.
I kicked at the wild understory, struck
with a brass-tipped cane
I keep against the fearsome serpents,
but was defeated by the resistant thicket
and the stout tangle of vines.
When Capitao Gonzales came to my shouts,
behind him the lovely Rosa, her servants,
I urged them back, mixing what Portuguese I have—
Batente! Stop! Por favor! And when I turned

again, the monster and its delicate prey,
now beyond every hope, had vanished into the dark
that spread, untrammeled, along the base
of the jumble-green cliff.

The Origami Hummingbirds

The American painter Martin Johnson Heade
in Rio de Janeiro, November 10, 1863

I go to the *Candelaria,*
to bargain for hummingbird skins.

I want the skins of Woodnymphs, of Star Throats;
perhaps a Frilled Coquette.

I find the stall of a feather merchant—
an ancient from Macao—his skins laid

among Toucan and Parrot skins; the plumes
of Macaws, Quetzals, and Elegant Trogans.

Here are Hermits and Emeralds,
there—Thorntails, the Snowcaps, and Topaz.

The words are hard, but I haggle
eight skins for a few *Reals* each.

I watch his wife fold squares of parchment
into tiny hummingbirds.

Her fingers move quickly, like the birds
she forms—creamy paper shifted

in valleys and rifts, by halves and back-folds—
the parchment reversed, crimped and fanned

into the shape of a hummer, one paused to sip
sweet nectar. In a final twist, she forms

the beak, and, with a flourish of hands,
lays the body on the table.

She has filled a blue bowl with these,
and for a *centavo* each, I buy six.

At home, I hang five near the window;
from the yard, cut sprays of honey flowers, tie them

among the squadron of hummingbirds, and watch
as birds and blossoms dance in the evening breeze.

I pour a tumbler of rye, and shape
the body of the sixth paper hummingbird,

my hands trying, without success,
to know the very heart of it.

A Study of Rosa Gonzales

-The American painter Martin Johnson Heade
in Rio de Janeiro, November 16, 1863

I was working on my canvas of the Starthroats, hoping to catch the red chest of the male—the shift from the deeply shaded right, to left (lighter, a rose madder). When tired of this, I would dab at the landscape which rests upon my larger easel, or step onto the porch, among the leaves and passion flowers, searching out a movement of air and watching a slice of roadway, just visible through the trees. Around four, I heard the latch close, and turned to find Rosa Gonzales, her back pressed to the door. Her dark hair was pinned and she wore a blue skirt and muslin blouse. I had not known she was back from Petropolis. When asked how she had slipped away from her servants, she smiled slightly and shrugged. I offered a glass of claret and went back to work. She held the wine glass near her face as she circled the room, wordlessly inspecting the landscape, my sketchbook open at the table, the hummingbird studies drying along the wall, glancing at the disarray of my bed.

She asked, Had I ever painted the human body? Yes, I said, brush in hand, touching a hummer's tail, I had once made a life as a portrait painter in America. But the naked form, she asked. *Despido.* Had I painted many unclothed women? I said I had painted a model years ago while in Rome; that such things were not often done in my country. She asked, Would I like to paint her unclothed? The room became silent. Outside, the birds and insects stilled. I would first need to make sketches, I said. She nodded, pulled the pin from her hair, and stepped behind the lacquered screen. I laid the blue-flowered coverlet across the rosewood chair, moved it toward the light of the west window, and when she came out, pushed her gently down. Her black hair fell thickly about her shoulders, her skin was everywhere a pale luminous brown, her breasts thick, her nipples, dark mahogany knots. The tendrils of her sex matched that of her head. I asked her to pull her right leg loosely to her breast, arranged my chair to face her directly, wondered at the wildness in her eyes, and began.

Orpheus, Gathering the Trees

The Metamorphoses of Ovid, Book X,
Lines 86-110

When love died the second time,
he sang at dawn in the empty field
and the trees came to listen.
A little song for the tag alder,
the fire cherry, the withe-willow—
the simple-hearted ones that come quickly
to loneliness.
Then he sang for the mulberry
with its purple fruit,
for the cedar and the tamarack.
He sang *bel canto* for the quaking aspen
and the stave oak;
something lovely for the white pine,
the fever tree, the black ash.
From the air, he called the sparrows
and the varieties of wrens.
Then he sang for a bit of pestilence—
for the green caterpillars,
for the leaf worms and bark beetles.
Food to suit the flickers and the crows.
So that, in the wood lot,
there would always be empty places.
So he would still know loss.

Flying Down to Rio (1933)

Yankee ingenuity and a little rule bending save the Hotel Atlantico. Unable to obtain the proper entertainment permit for the hotel, [Fred Astaire] stages the opening day show, with its contingent of beautiful girls, on the wings of airplanes above the hotel rather than in it. The ingenious Yankee Clippers save Belinha's father's hotel from the scheming "buzzards," and Roger Bond marries Belinha. Thus the film has reassured audiences that North and South America can live in harmony, with mutual respect and well-intentioned assistance when needed.
    -Rosalie Schwartz, *Flying Down to Rio: Hollywood, Tourists, and Yankee Clippers* (2004), p. 14

"What have these South Americans got below the equator that we haven't?"
    -The actress Mary Korman in *Flying Down to Rio*

When Fred Astaire *glissandos* through the saxophones
on the hotel's marbled deck, waves his hand, and is seen

by Ginger Rogers, high above, astride the Sopwith Camel,
Ginger gives a sign, and the biplanes—

the Staggerwing, the Ikarus Aero,
the Fairey Swordfish—buzz the Hotel Atlantico.

The girls windmill their arms, their legs kick right
then left, as Fred croons and the band plays "Flying Down to Rio."

No, there are no hummingbirds, though the second unit
filmed some in Brazil, thinking the birds—flitting,

sipping orchids—could be fade-cut to the girls,
dancing atop the wings.

But in the final print, we have only moonlight, an elaborate
dance—"the Caroica"—in which lovers tango, sharing

the knowledge of their bodies, forehead
to forehead; the thrum of those great noisy engines,

a few sweet songs, and the frantic, prop-washed girls, tapping
and wheeling, far above the sugar plum beach.

The Hummingbird Artist
Dreams of the Ladder of Heaven

> Sunday evening, I attended a lecture at The American Union given by
> the Reverend Fletcher on the Book of Genesis and the works of the
> English naturalist, Charles Darwin. Spent a fitful night, possessed by
> strange, recurring dream.
> > -From the Notebooks of the American painter Martin Johnson
> > Heade in Rio de Janeiro, November 27, 1863

> He dreamed, and behold a ladder set up on the earth, and the top of it
> reached to heaven: and behold the angels of God ascending and descending...
> > -Genesis 28:12

A golden ladder, behold—
a ladder stepped with thirty rungs.
Written on four was *Renounce the World,*
and these were coiled with woody vines;
with anacondas and jeweled snakes.
And laced throughout—hummingbirds—
Ruby Throats and Violet Ears, sipping
at rain lilies and the bluets of the understory.

Above, steps five through seven,
upon which was written *Penitence and Affliction.*
There the Thorntails, raveling along the selvage,
circled the Frilled Coquettes, and drank from gardenias
braided through the golden rungs. And all the air—
redolent of candles, from which a musk-like honey
had never quite been lost.

Rungs numbered eight though seventeen—
a long run of golden steps—inscribed
The Defeat of Vice and Acquisition of Virtue,
by which the birds meant—for in this dream,

he understood their songs—slander, greed, and lust.
Here, Woodnymphs arced with
Sappho Comets, and through the steps
turned passion flowers—their stamens and pistils
despairing—laid open for all to see.

Aroused, he woke and went naked to the veranda.
He looked to the moonlit garden
and the dark of the breadfruit tree, that flowed
like a river, down from the midnight sky.

Called to sleep again, he dreamed steps eighteen
through twenty-six, each of which was honey-gold,
and written there—*The Sins of Loneliness.*
Round these hovered Golden Throats and Sun Gems,
ravening at the sweet of wild indigo.

And he dreamed—was it blasphemy
to dream this?—*If I cannot do what God is doing,
I must steal what God is doing.*

So rose the twenty-seventh, twenty-eighth,
and twenty-ninth steps, upon which was written
Peace of the Soul. There the Streamertails
spiraled among the Plovercrests, and all
of them, male and female, fell upon the columbine
and flame azaleas, while above these, the thirtieth rung—
swaled with clouds, dissolving and re-forming.

And beyond this, *Oh*, a fiery gold,
suffusing the stairway in light.

Thorntails, Brazil (1863-1864)

[Martin Johnson Heade's hummingbirds] are the very image of Eden.
-Theodore Stebbins

Brownish-green, illumined, fragile—
she settles on the twiggy nest.

See the leaves that form a parasol. Her mate,
with his green chest and forked tail, faces left.

The depths are greeny dark. A mist rises,
forming clouds, clouds. There is a moment

of lassitude; a soul-stillness that
foretells rain. *Thorntails*—their tails split

like serpents' tongues. But where is the bittersweet—
the bitten fruit, a single drop of blood?

Here is Eden, not yet cursed, though the one
who named these knew something of loss.

The cup of the nest, the female covering.
The word *beauty* held out, with its empty palm.

At the Cavern of Winged Echoes

The American painter Martin Johnson Heade in Brazil,
December 6, 1863

…Heav'n hides nothing from thy view,
Nor the deep Tract of Hell.
                    -John Milton, Paradise Lost, Book I, lines 27-28

West of Rio some forty miles—
sketching, gathering skins.
Our party, Capitao Gonzales and I walk a creek,
overhung with vines, festooned with passion flowers
and gardenias. The air is gummy hot;
the glowering sky, seldom glimpsed through the trees.
We have seen parrots of all sorts, cockatoos,
a female tapir and its squealing, slick-furred young,
come to water to drink. Our guide
finds jaguar tracks along the muddy path.
Perhaps it is that great cat's roar, faintly heard,
that lays back the ears of my donkey,
that stills the monkeys' cries.

The creek ends at a water-lilied pool, by a vast rise
of lichened rock, and there stands
a naked man; a native—bowl cut hair,
his red skin bruised with tattoos,
mournfully playing an ocarina.
He faces darkness, where the stream flows
from the cliff. Capitao Gonzales raises a hand
and we still. He points at a gnarled tree
just across the pool, where a pair of hummingbirds—the female,
bronze, nearly invisible in the low light, the male,
green chested, sort the air around a nest.

The Captain points to the female, then to me.
He will take the male. We raise our fowling guns
and in the instant before our shots ring out,
there is but the sound of the native,
blowing a note on his strange flute.
The hummers drop and the red man
disappears into the forest.

The birds are White-vented Violet Ears—
I know as much from Gould's volume—good specimens,
despite the touch of dust shot.
A black youth scrambles for the nest,
and to my regret, finds two hatchlings—
pinkish brown, wiggling
about; waiting, as ever, to be fed.

I wring their necks and place the nest
in my leather satchel.

We make camp on the shores of the pool
and while our porters set up tents,
fashion a torch from rags and lamp-oil.
Capitao Gonzales and I, bent nearly double,
wade through the maw of the cave.
Darkness yawns into a dark lake, and rises
to a cathedral of limestone, a Pandemonium
of eerie stalactites and dripping water.
Every sound—our astonishments,
our whispers—comes back to us
in echoes, until the cavern echoes
with incomprehensible voices,

deepening, more strange than our bizarre mix
of Portuguese and English.

For dinner—roast fish speared from the pool,
passion fruit, a bit of cognac sipped from tin cups.

At true dusk, we hear a hellish symphony, slowly
building—a high pitched scree, as of Bedlamite violinists,
striking bows across strings, growing
in intensity and volume.
Then a cloud of bats, flying as if to the call
of Satan himself, explodes from the cave,
skirls round our fire, and rises along the creek.
Black wings blot out the last embers of sun
and the cries of our men, who wail
and cross themselves, until the scarf-black horde
vanishes, into a tall bewingéd dark.

Two Sun Gems on a Branch (1864-1865)

The American painter Martin Johnson Heade

Beak to beak, face to face, green body to green body.
What she says, startles him—flares his keyboard tail,
the yellow tufts above his ears. Along the branch,
the burst of a yellow flower. Gray clouds here,
a touch of blue on the upper left. The twisty vines,
the Spanish moss—all hang, exhausted, from the trees.

These two have no nest. Perhaps, there will never be a nest.
What grief does she speak—broken hearted or afraid?
With his flaming head tufts, he could be Moses, come down
Sinai, as Michelangelo had him—transfigured.
But these hummers have a lesser narrative:
We must live for love and not for sorrow.

I have made a small place. Night comes
and day goes. In half-light, our branch will be just-so.

Two Hummingbirds with their Young (1864)

The American painter Martin Johnson Heade

It is the last painting in a series of three
in which the Red-tailed Comets have not moved—
the female, alighted left (long tail, white tip),
the male, posed right (longer tail, black tip).
But at last, the chicks have hatched
and two tiny beaks—in the others
there was but one egg—wait to be fed.
There are changes. The nest, hanging
mid-canvas, is ragged. The branch supporting
the hummingbirds—net handle to the hanging nest—
is thinner, more attenuate. In his notebook,
Heade penciled the colors of these birds
onto his sketch: "metallic green"
at the throats, "crimson" across their backs.
Over time, done in oils, these colors have faded—
the brightest lights are often fugitive.
But see the sky—how the scumbled clouds
have pared from canvas to canvas.
The clouds are now a buffered orange, suggesting
cut mango. The hills and Spanish moss
reflect the day to come.
Look quickly. Comets cannot hold for long.
There are gnats to be gathered and nectar
to sip from yellow trumpet flowers.
All day, gaping mouths will trace this light
around the cup of the nest.

Hummingbirds Near a Volcano (1864-1865)

The American painter Martin Johnson Heade

Is the volcano, rising in the distance, dangerous?
It belches smoke, threatens fire, the ash billows off
to the right. But no; even in the orange sky, which
may mean flames—or sunrise—the birds see no threat.
The male hummer, with its navy-blue head, puffs
his white chest; shows the underside of his tail.
The female, emerald-brown, less a sight than him—
sees her mate and fans her tail (green, white).

Because I love you, I no longer fear disaster, though
there is always something (cancer, my weak heart)
puttering in the distance. The mountain is dark, there
is ash. But we can fly, and orchids and epiphytes
taste sweet. The palm fronds are lush; those two clouds,
nearly diaphanous. And this branch we perch upon
seems sturdy enough, for now.

Field Notes on *The Black-Breasted Plovercrest* (1864-1865)

The American painter Martin Johnson Heade near Tangua, Brazil,
December 14, 1863

His chest glows purple, the nest is flecked with gold.
I'll paint the sky a stormy gray—a patch or two of blue.
How does the nest remain in place, how certain is its hold?

The yellow crest atop his head! Amazing to behold.
His mate is greenish-brown; I lost her when she flew.
His chest glows purple, the nest is flecked with gold.

Array them on a willow branch? It seems a strong foothold.
Mist comes across the hills. The furthest fade from view.
I sketch one egg within the nest, uncertain of its hold.

Those dots—below the nest—are dabs of marigold.
The clouds along the upper left—a shade quite near ecru.
His chest glows purple, the nest is flecked with gold.

They pose as I found them; more naturally than Gould's.
These days in the jungle will prove my work's virtue.
How does the nest remain in place, how certain is its hold?

These Plovercrests are rare so close to Rio I am told.
I sketched as quickly as I could, and tried to note each hue—
His chest glows purple, the nest is flecked with gold.
How can the nest remain in place, how certain is its hold?

Orpheus Considers His Approach to Cerberus

A three-headed dog named Cerberus guards
the opposite shore of Styx, ready to devour
living intruders or ghostly fugitives.
-Robert Graves, *The Greek Myths,* 31.a

As one comes to wolves. Song of canine bodies
circling through the pines. Aria of bone-gnaw,
of driven snow in Caucasus, of sweet, sweet marrow.
Song of lip-curl, of bloody gums, of gritted teeth and snarl.
Whimpered song of bitch-and-den, song of musk,
of tongued pups, of burrow thick with steam.
Song of fire, circle song, beaten onto skins. Song of meat,
of shearling, of ashy coals and cinders, song of hellish fleas.
Ballad of hound-hunger, of want; song that calms the dog.

In the stony deep, Oh! are lesser gods, the stink of sulphur,
and the spirits of the dead. The beast is chained, or else
the beast runs loose. I have sung my way through darkness
and wait upon the shore with open palms.
Dog, dog, dog. What song must I sing to get by thee?

Notes of Capitao Eduardo Gonzales
in Preparation for a Report to
His Excellency Baron de Temandere,
First Admiral and Commander of the Brazilian
Imperial Navy, Regarding the Activities of
the American Painter, Martin Johnson Heade

Rio de Janeiro, December 17, 1863

He came with graphite and oils, to paint hummingbirds.
A ghost, he walks among orchids, seeking hummingbirds.

He has filled his room with easels, chairs, a wicker bed.
He scrawls upon foolscap, the floor awash in hummingbirds.

At night he drinks red wine, Bourbon and port.
He speaks with his hands; his fingers—like hummingbirds.

He cuts passion flowers, gardenias and palm fronds.
Near each, he lays the bodies of hummingbirds.

I have rounded the Cape, and know many lands.
Ceylon was most strange. I remember no hummingbirds.

He supports the Union cause, and freedom for our slaves.
He does not love war. He loves only hummingbirds.

Women come to him so freely.
Is my sister lost among his hummingbirds?

I saw him sketch the harbor; our stone fortress.
He knows no peace. He wants only hummingbirds.

A dead-shot with a fowling gun. He abhors
the blood, as he works to skin hummingbirds.

My agents have trailed him at night.
He seldom sleeps, and dreams of hummingbirds.

I find him with his sketchbook, staring at the trees.
He says the palms, the banyans are alive with hummingbirds.

In the steamy mountains he steps from a mist.
Cradling his sketchbook, babbling of hummingbirds.

For a week the rain was never-ending.
I found him singing scales, cooing, "I am a hummingbird!"

I imagine their breasts—gold and green and red.
I fear I too will dream of *colibris.*

His leather satchel keeps his most secret things—
the merkins of their tiny nests, the bodies of his hummingbirds.

There are days I yearn for the sea. The sea was
all I knew, before the days of hummingbirds.

I will go with him to the borderlands.
He says the cobalt sky will swell with hummingbirds.

I remain your servant, Eduardo Gonzales—
Captain of the Imperial Navy, *escrivao* of hummingbirds.

Insomnia, with Sappho Comet

The American painter Martin Johnson Heade
in Petropolis, Brazil, January 6, 1864

It is midnight, the time is going by,
and I sleep alone.
                    -Sappho

The banyans give way in a rising wind—
the whirr of insects, their buzzy-ness, batters
the mosquito net. Night, and I have seen
the last of the carriages, heard the last
spongy vowels of Portuguese.
Boa noite, my loves.
I rise again, then go back to bed.
No clarity yet from the moon, the stars.
I have lived like this for weeks—night-walker,
insensate, as if soul-numbed
by the black man's *macumba*.
All day, I study the cliffs
(viridian, cobalt green); the canopy of trees
that, seen from below, goes dark
and consumes the sky.

I have sketched both leaf and bark,
root and vine—the orchids, magnolias,
acacias—flowers that burst from tree-trunks,
the ochre of ground cover, every creeping yellow flower.
The Sappho Comets elude. I watch the vines,
sure the birds must nest within them;
walk for days to find their tiny hearts
beating in the jungle-dark.

I imagine a fuzzy pudenda of nest
adrift on a golden river,
have seen the skins, razored from their ribs,
for sale near the Cathedral—
pale green throats, brown wings, the long split
tails (crimson and brown, the females just tipped
with white), the nearly terra cotta breasts.

Tonight at the home of Ambassador Webb
I drank a glass of Comet Wine—
a Sauterne, resinously ambered,
the famous Chateau d'Yquem, from 1811.
He said that as Earth whirled across the comet's tail,
Bordeaux was sown with comet dust,
and the vineyards were restored.
At dinner, in wine-light, among the silver candlesticks,
the women were so beautiful.
Of stars and their miraculous histories,
I know too little. And so this prayer: Sappho Comets,
flitting, hovering; poet whispering couplets
from her elliptic ball of ice, looping for eons
around the burning Sun—let me sleep,
then lead me back, silently, to life.
Boa noite, my loves.
In the garden, the full moon pauses
and shudders across the pond.

Field Notes: January 30, 1864

The American painter Martin Johnson Heade near Petropolis

Spanish moss, slate gray

Sky—dolphin gray and satin steel

Red passion flower, opening,
pistil erect

Sun Gem—
Blue head,
emerald green,
gold ear feathers flaring, dark under-
tail curled beneath
the vine

—Sappho Comet
Garnet back,
(rose madder over white?) green
head, yellow
throat, long
scissored
tail

A world, all tender and awry.

I will never know these flaming passion flowers.

Fire Down Below (1957)

"There are all kinds of rumors about me, and they're all true. You can make some up if you want."
                    -Robert Mitchum

Irwin Shaw's original screenplay had been constructed around a framing device. The [Ulysses] is about to blow up, and a man—the Jack Lemon character—is trapped…As the trapped man waits to be rescued, his story is told in flashbacks. For the finale, the story returns to the burning boat and the Mitchum character's last minute rescue of his former pal. The producers cut this structure to make the narrative linear and supposedly did a number of other things of which director [Robert] Parrish disapproved. Whether or not there was a better film hiding behind the producer's re-edit, what went into release was not much—pretty to watch but empty and disconnected at the center.
                    -Lee Server, *Robert Mitchum: "Baby, I Don't Care"* (2001)

It is as if the painter had climbed into the trees to witness a scene both intimate and grand, one that is highly charged with natural energy.
                    -Theodore Stebbins, Jr., *Martin Johnson Heade* (1999)

I assemble the hummingbird feeder—
affix a frame to the handblown glass,
thread strings that will hang in the eaves,
mix the nectar—four parts water, one
sugar—thinking about the film, how it breaks
in disparate halves. The smugglers—Tony,
played by Jack Lemon, the surly Felix
played by Robert Mitchum—agree to ferry
the mysterious Irena (Rita Hayworth)
to the isle of Santa Nada, no questions asked.
Is Irena running from the Russians
or the Americans? It's never made clear.
Even the guide calls this "a long, confused story."
The boat stops for Mardi Gras,
and Rita, gone from the screen for years,

kicks off her shoes and mambos for Felix—
she cannot take her eyes from him—
but when he tries to kiss her,
she will not give herself, saying only,
"I am waiting for someone to touch me with kindness."
Saint Nothing.
Not even our stars can make it right.

The feeder, once hung, skews left.
Misshapen at its core, unglued,
the glass drains of all sweetness.
I re-assemble the body—
apply a smear of tanglefoot,
so nectar is not hoarded by ants.
I narrow the feeding holes,
so hornets cannot swarm the glass.
Should I hang the feeder out along the roof line,
near the day lilies and nasturtiums, not far
from the loosestrife and sedge?
The glue on my index fingers, my thumbs,
sticks; makes perfect, skin-like fingerprints.
I am hoping the birds will come.

Months go by with the cast in Tobago.
They stay at the Blue Haven Hotel, drinking zombies.
Rita rips her fan mail into pieces
and throws them in the sea.
Mitchum, when not hacking through mangroves
searching for *yohimbe* bark—the savage, dreamed-of
aphrodisiac—falls in love with calypso,
crawling on-stage to pound the congas

and warble "Little Bird,"
and "What Is This Generation Coming To?"
While Jack Lemmon, our poor befuddled Jack,
finds a painting in the lobby—
Fighting Hummingbirds with Pink Orchid—
by an American he's never heard of, and falls in love
with the hummingbirds of Tobago—
the Black-throated Mangoes, the Emeralds,
the Hermits and Blue Sapphires.

At night, he cracks a fifth of rum
and tops off the feeders, hanging them out
among the gloriosas and hibiscus,
noting the colors of the birds, until
Mitchum, beyond stinko, wings an ash tray at Jack,
smashing a dining room window.
Amid the shards of glass, the lobster bisque
and turtle soup, the screaming guests
and tipped-over cymbals, Mitchum feints
as three sailors swing wildly, and all of them—
the sailors, our stars, the rhythm section
from the band—tumble into the pool, while Rita,
oblivious, a pink orchid pinned in her
luxuriant red hair, dances—barefoot and alone—
to a tune of crashing bottles, to a song
of curses, of spilled rum and shattered glass.

By Oil Lamp, Martin Johnson Heade
Decants a Glass of Madeira and Contemplates
Hooded Visorbearer (1864-1865)

Rio de Janeiro, February 6, 1864

"What do you see?"
                        -Mark Rothko

Let the vermilion wine, so dark along its edge,
color my brush, so his tail will fan in every red—

at least one plume, true to the color of blood.
Let pollen spot the leaves in the silver rain.

Let jacaranda anchor to the hill, and may its roots,
laced through the urinous loam, hold its place

against the torrent. Leaves and gray epiphytes
dwarf the tiny birds. Not sowing, not reaping, not

gathering into barns. In the lower right, sunlight comes—
(scarlet lake, orange cadmium). She is green, her eye

not truly a bird's eye, but that of a woman. Should I
change it? I cannot change it. Let the fire

of my tongue go on, singing through my hand.
Because we live, what follows must be the afterlife.

Orfeu Negro (1959)

A young beauty in white [Eurydice] disembarks from a ferry [in Rio de Janeiro], is startled by a blind peddler. Her agitation seems naive, an innocent overwhelmed by the ubiquitous carnival drumming and the dangerous festive vibe of the swarming revelers in the harbour region.
-Lawrence Russell, *Black Orpheus* (2002)

Call the blind man in the first scene Tiresias,
after the sightless oracle
who knew the language of birds;
for that is his role when her boat nudges
the dock, not far from the Cathedral.
On his staff, he carries a spray of pinwheels—
green, orange, red—they could be
a bough of hummingbirds—spinning.
Eurydice flees the masked figure of Death.
Because he is a soothsayer, the blind man knows
this, and says, "I can feel your heart
beating—like a trapped bird."
He gives her a necklace of honey flowers
To help her forget, and points the way to safety,
though she is soon lost among the dancers,
the fish mongers and butchers of the marketplace.
Our camera finds her, wandering near the bird sellers,
where ravens (for they, too, are Death)
crowd a yellow hummingbird, lying at the bottom
of a wrought iron cage.

Orpheus Speaks

The American painter Martin Johnson Heade
in Petropolis, Brazil

Carnaval, February 10, 1864

In the ballroom I held a lyre,
and wore the masque
of those bereft of speech.
As we danced the *anglaise,*
I watched your humid eyes,
the turn of your fan.
Your masque was pale,
your dress a creamy white;
your shawl, black velvet—
a shroud for one
lost to the world above.
I was leaving the underworld, and yes,
believed that you would follow.
From the iron gate (gargoyles
and the curl of hammered leaves—
the hiss of gaslights), I looked back,
and watched as you turned from me,
like a frightened bird
who knows only the call
of a dark and stony place.

The Response of Eurydice

Rosa Gonzales in Petropolis, Brazil

Carnaval, February 10, 1864

Two orchids were my laurels.
I wore the masque
of one who is truly lost.
As we danced,
the tenderness you sought
I bowed and tried to give.
In another place, what seemed
another time, we had loved.
Do you think I did not remember?
I was to follow you, no matter
that everyone would watch me go.
But as you turned to look
I saw only a caped body,
twisted iron, and the empty glow of lights.
I knew that night is fire,
that the days to come
would turn to ash.
And still, I burned for you.
Yes, I knew the flames.

Studies for *The Blue Morpho* (1864)

The American painter Martin Johnson Heade at the Rio Iguacu Falls,
February 24, 1864

Blue—a startling blue in full sunlight
and large as the human hand. The edges,
limned by a chocolate brown, are nearly black
when the wings are stretched,
pinned against a sheet of creamy parchment.
The children dip their hands in indigo
and flutter them at the tourists, singing out
in Portuguese. For a few coins,
they will take you to fields blue with butterflies
off the many paths leading to the Falls.
Capitao Gonzales, resplendent in his naval jacket
and spit-black boots, waves them off
and the children fall back—they know
only the sleepy provincial guards—it is rare
to see a naval officer this far upriver.
Our guide is a dark man—depicted here—
who employs two daughters in his work.
The girls tie scraps of shiny blue cloth
to long sticks and wave them like flags
in the deep green clearings. The Morphos
come ready to fight—for mates,
territory, food—they are not so different from us.
In his best English, our guide says the mist
weighs upon the butterflies' wings;
makes them easier to catch.
He nets twelve males, stuns them, butterfly-by-butterfly,
in jars of deadly naphtha. Before dinner,
I pin them out—note the chocolate undersides,

how the satiny blue changes to black
as the wings are turned in lantern-light.
I sketch their wings and bodies
on a sheaf of fine vellum—
carefully, from different angles,
as I remember them in life—at rest on a vine
or bougainvillea, drying their wings
slowly in the humid air, then in full-flight,
darting round the guide's daughters,
as the girls wave their satin flags.
Mixing the paint will be a challenge—
the precise blend of silver-gray and Delft-blue,
also the fine vein-work of their wings; the way
a blue pane goes black
as blue is turned from the sun.
And the Falls dazzle us—silver
and white, raveling down over numerous
cataracts, the air filled with mist,
the cliffs jeweled with all manner of wildflowers,
Cattleya orchids and jungle greens.
Here, I have drawn us, taking a pirogue
through a less turbulent pool.
Dinner is *alcatra* and grilled fish,
two bottles of good Argentinian wine,
cigars and the company of Capitao Gonzales.
As has become our custom, we drink often
to the Emperor's health, though I cannot stop
turning my hand in candlelight,
wondering at the darkness
as I close and open my palm.

Sun Gems (ca. 1864-1865)

Location Unknown
-*The Life and Work of Martin Johnson Heade:*
A Critical Analysis and Catalog Raisonné
by Theodore Stebbins, Jr., (2000), p. 286

Nothing remains as it was.
Who can say it should be otherwise?
In another life, I walked with a woman I loved
through an orchard in New Hampshire
in which 10,000 fireflies—Yes, I saw but did not
count them—blinked off-and-on in the trees.
Things remain at risk—this green earth, our lives.
We know fireflies from the stars only because
the stars have never left us. Years ago,
the forest in which these hummingbirds lived
was razed for mahogany and rosewood.
Now the land is gouged in muddy terraces,
where 1,000 men—here is a photograph—
dig each day, scratching deeper and deeper for gold.
When it rains, the flood cannot be raised
from its depths. What should we save—
a fallen world, or the life we are finally given to live?

Of his lost canvas, we know something of how it looks.
How the Sun Gems were posed—face-to-face,
their green and creamy bodies, the piano-key flare
of their tails, the tufts of orange, fused to each side
of the male's head. Imagine the oil light, luminous
and tender, within which the painter worked,
his palette—the thin shingle upon which
the peony red, the lamp-black, the oxides of
cinnabar, were smeared and mixed.

He worked for days on a single red flower, then
turned to the Spanish moss, hung languidly from the trees.
The female seems to say, *In a secret place,*
let us hide our love for 100 years.

It's All True (1942)

Even the reconstructed portions of "Jangadeiros" (the only fully recon-
structed episode) shown in the 1993 documentary, function as just such
a synecdoche: "now that you have seen this, you can just imagine what
the rest is like."
                          -Catherine L. Benamou,
                          Orson Welles's Pan American Odyssey, p. 66

Peter Bogdonovich: Well, it's usually used against you; "some kind of
drunken orgy."

Orson Welles: Yeah, I know, but nobody was drunk at all. It was a lunch
party, you know—middle of the afternoon. Just terribly high spirited.
                          -*This is Orson Wells*, p. 161

"[Martin Johnson Heade's landscape paintings] may be of some interest
to Middle Americans; I would expect to see one hanging in a parlor in
Ohio or Illinois. His hummingbirds are of less interest. Perhaps one
could find them decorating a hut in Brazil."
                          -The landscape painter Albert Bierstadt (1869)

No one knows the whole truth. There are mostly nega-
tives—some say 100,000 feet—buried in a vault in Cen-
tury City; what some studio big-shot called "reels of sweaty
natives jumping up and down," perhaps thirty complete
minutes of Carnival, another ten of Bonito the Courageous
Bull, and forty minutes on the odyssey of the *Jangadeiros,*
those brave, doomed fishermen.

ii

There was no script. Only a "Dream Book"—margin doo-
dles, Orson's elliptic scribbles, notes of what might have
been—"The Story of Jazz" sent churning up the Mississip-
pi, the immigrant tale of an Italian bricklayer, a starvation
narrative set among the Eskimos, Pizarro's lonely conquest

44

of Peru. It was to be "a night full of cinema," it was to tell "The Big Truths," and rally a hemisphere against the Nazi menace, but when the money went— *poof!*—Orson and his second unit drank and danced through Carnival—its theme that desperate war year, "Let us party before we die,"—smoking dope, sniffing ether, chasing girls with seltzer bottles, drinking the last Chateau Lafite in Brazil.

iii

When the *macumba* priest, unpaid, muttered a curse, and drove a feathered spike through the "Dream Book," and RKO sent a Pan Am Clipper to claim the cameras, Orson hid some black-and-white film, sworn to finish the tale of the fishermen, though even that would end in disaster, when the biblical Leviathan, fighting the colossal squid, rose from the bay—foaming, spuming—and slurped down the fabled Jacare, Ahab of the *Jangadeiros*. Or so Orson said.

iv.

On his last day in Rio, planning to dodge his landlord's claim for damages, Orson hosts a boozy lunch for Alfonso Reyes, a poet from Mexico, whose work you've never read, because so little exists in English—not his *Yerbas del Tarahumara*, not his *Homero en Cuernavaca*.

v.

They drink *mojitos*. They smoke *figurados*. Orson groans about his greedy landlord. Alfonso looks about. The chairs, the fuzzy red couch, the dressing screen—all seem fine to him. The poet pronounces the landlord "a Nazi, ridiculous, a thief!" Alfonso shouts, "Death to those who impede the fight against *Fascismo!* Let's *really* break something!" The poet lifts the coffee table, trots to the veranda, and tosses it into the street. Orson grabs a lamp and throws it after the table.

vi.

If everything is damaged, everything must go—and the continuity girl, the gaffer, the beach-boy turned best-boy—everyone begins to throw things—a side chair, the bed, the *armoire*, a box of smoked fish.

vii.

A crowd gathers outside the apartment. Orson toasts Brazil, he makes a rambling speech from the veranda. "Death to *Fascistas!*" The *Cariocas* cheer as forks, pans and Depression ware—"Made in Japan!" Orson roars—crash onto the boulevard.

viii.

At last, there is only a small, dark painting—two hummingbirds, face-to-face in a rain forest. Their bodies are green and creamy, their tails flare. Alfonso holds the paintings at arm's length, thinks, *Si*, the tails are piano keys! He notes the tufts of orange, fused, like lightning bolts, at each side of the male's head. Lovely, but no matter. He throws the painting over. And because it's true, Yes, because it's all true, the canvas sails and loops to the street, where a small boy lifts it from the splintered furniture, and runs—see here, in this photograph—toward a shack upon the hill.

Letter to Professor Louis Agassiz,
Posted with the Harbor Pilot,
Rio de Janeiro

The American painter Martin Johnson Heade, April 4, 1864

Only a look and a voice, then darkness again and a silence.
-Henry Wadsworth Longfellow

May this note welcome your brigantine—
I regret we shall pass at sea.
Tonight, I sail with my hummingbirds
and six Brazilian landscapes,
with funding to lithograph my *Gems*
on the great presses of England, in a book
meant to charm connoisseurs
and naturalists as well. I have unraveled myself,
working to portray these splendid birds
as I found them in this habitat,
with every attention given to detailing the hummers
and the vagaries of flora—epiphytes,
passion flowers, orchids, vines—
within which I recorded their manners and lives.

When we met in Boston, you asked that I gather
100 hummingbird eggs, to assist you
in documenting the birds of Amazonia.
Sadly, the elusiveness of these hummers—
their eccentric natures, et cetera,—their habits
of nesting high in the cloud-thick cover,
and my reluctance, in several cases,
to disturb the domestic lives
of these lovely birds, made it impossible
to meet the larger part of your request.

I have, however, left three tiny eggs for you
with the Honorable James Monroe, American Consul
in Rio, with a complete record of their species
and the circumstances under which they were found.
One, you will see, is a caramel-brown; one
rose-colored and speckled; one
the most astonishing sky-blue
likely to be found on this continent.

Donald Duck in Brazil

Saludos Amigos (1942)

The Three Caballeros (1944)

Clown of the Jungle (1947)

Not everyone was enamored of this new direction. James Agee detected a "streak of cruelty" in *Caballeros*, a streak he thought had been gathering force for years in Disney's films, perhaps as Walt's retributions for the tribulations he felt he had suffered. Barbara Deming, writing in the Partisan Review, also believed that Disney "had wrought something monstrous," but she thought that in doing so he had made a telling commentary on the times. As Deming saw it, Disney's "gift" was to "be able to accept wholeheartedly the outlook of the hour, and to improvise with it, whatever it might be."...In *Caballeros*, by making the entire film into a phantasmagoria in which characters and shapes keep morphing into other characters and shapes, in which the object of one's desire seems to be attained only to disappear, in which both characters and the audience seems to lose their bearings, Walt Disney had managed to find the perfect metaphor for a world lost in the vortex of war. "Nothing holds its shape," Deming observed, concluding that Donald Duck in *Caballeros* "could be likened in his adventures here, his confusions and translations, to most major characters now passing across our screens" and presumably to Americans generally: lost.

-Neal Gabler, *Walt Disney: The Triumph of The American Imagination* (2007), pp. 409-410

Something strange is creeping across me.
-John Ashbery

I was the yang to Mickey's sweet yin.
I was the acolyte of Walt's cold, black heart—
his bag man, wingman, his
second-story man, his confidential agent.
Follow the money, amigo; dig deep.
I had clearance from J. Edgar himself.
In 1941, Walt and I and a few trusty sketchers
flew to Rio on a "Goodwill Tour." Truth is,

we went to fight the Nazi menace.
While the others noshed *risoles* and drew pretty pictures,
the dirty work—the shiv jobs, the mail drops,
the passing of unmarked *dolares* in *preto* briefcases—
was handled by me.

Okay, I schtupped the Samba Queen.
And if I grease-gunned the Araquan bird
in the *Clown of the Jungle* sequence—
the one the studio suppressed
until after the war—what of it?
I killed the clown in order to save him.
I was filming four blue hummingbirds
who idled in the acacia tree, crooning
zum, zum, zum, so sweetly to the flowers.
I finally couldn't stand the Araquan's popping
into the view finder; his constant *chaca-laca-laca.*
My job was to show those *Cariocas* that, if push
came to nut-crunch, it was *our* hemisphere, too.
Call it friendly fire. Call it collateral damage, if you will.
In the steam of the steamy jungle, mistakes were made.
But there's no extradition deal with Brazil, and black ops
aren't covered by the Geneva Conventions.
No matter. These days, I'm an ex-pat, living in Belize.
The sun is bright, the *cerveza* cold, and nothing
can touch me but the breeze.

In Doldrums

The American painter Martin Johnson Heade
aboard the RMS *Oneida*, April 17, 1864

Twelve days out of Rio de Janeiro,
two since the wind fell.
The sails are furled and absent good air,
we go north under steam at nearly six knots.

At times a pod of dolphins rolls,
languorous, to our lee.

Last night at dinner, seated
with the Reverend MacLeod and his wife—
Presbyterians bound for Leeds
after preaching Hellfire across Brazil—
I spoke effusively of my hummingbird project,
and for my wit received a sermon
on the vanity of art, and from the wife,
a pointless tale of two dizzy Sun Gems
nesting near their mission house.
For these, I wonder,
was the word made flesh.

All morning the deckhands worked,
desultory in the sun.

I scribble towards a preface. Yet,
as the wind flagged, my zeal died with it,
and I wasted a day, enervated, shaded on the foredeck,
reading Coleridge—his poem of the albatross,
looped round the Mariner's neck

as penance—a sign—when his ship began to drift
among these latitudes.

Unbearable sun! Soot from the double stacks
settles 'cross the aft.

After leaving the MacLeods, I stood
smoking at the gunwale.
The stars were sprayed both North and South—
the sky, split in equatorial halves.
I saw the side-wheel churn
the phosphorescent water, the water
burning green and blue and white.
I went to my berth and unwrapped the skins
of two hummingbirds—
a Golden Throat, a Frilled Coquette—
and held them aloft, moving them
slowly up and down.
Formed as best I could into bodies—
the dead birds hovered, dove and flitted,
northing true around my head.

Orpheus, Adrift

> His head [the women] threw into the river,
> but it floated, still singing, down to the sea,
> and was carried to the island of Lesbos.
>   -Robert Graves, *The Greek Myths*, 28.d

Before my lips kissed the gravel
of river-bottom, I looked back

and saw the lost body,
and the fingers of my severed hand

twitching for the lyre.
Even then, I bobbed up, singing.

They threw the lyre beside me
and the lyre began to play.

I could hardly hear the strings
for the noise of rushing water.

As the river slowed through the tidal flats,
I came to love the taste of salt.

Eight months I have drifted
among the bluefish and the tunas.

Leeched of all blood and beset by sea lice,
one eye pecked by a passing gull—

I still sing. The lyre, drifting with me, plucks on.
I hear the sound of wave on beach

and sense the schooly candlefish,
frenzied by the surf.

Whatever land I drift toward,
I sing for what lives there.

My hair braids through the nut-brown kelp
that tangles along the shore.

The Apprentice Lithographer's Story

The American painter Martin Johnson Heade
in London, September 19, 1864

My name is Nigel. I am fifteen.
Two years have I worked at Day & Son,
Lithographers to Her Majesty, the Queen—
arriving at seven bells, cutting paper, grinding
inks; trolleying the gray siltstones
and barrels of gum arabic.

Allowed, once, to roll the sky
of a summer afternoon.

                              I've never met a man
like Martin Johnson Heade, have never seen
live hummingbirds, though he described them
for me—flitting, hovering; have never sketched birds
in a hot jungle, so different from the trees
near Lincoln's Inn. I cannot imagine
this place he calls *Bra-sil*.

These paintings of colorful birds, of
twisty green vines—or are they writhing serpents?—
of red and yellow flowers; they are so hard.
We ink stone after stone, align the register marks,
and cannot get them right. The draughtsmen
are befuddled; my master, Mr. Day, touches his
cheek, spotting it with ink. Mr. Heade rolls
his sleeves, stains his apron with crimson,
ochre, and blue, and still, by nightfall,
he shakes his head, *No*.

I was told to shear these proofs—a run of five—
but hid them in my bench, and spirited them away
after dark. Here, the birds are lovely,
but we have the sky too bright. Here we caught
the rainy sky, but could not strike the birds.
Were I sure of my colours, I could dab them
with water-tints, though I have seen Mr. Heade try
this, shaking his head No, no. In my room, I circle
the lithos about, look at each with one eye, then
the other; picturing these hummingbirds alive,
his rainy *Bra-sil* sky, abuzz with their wings.

Two Green Breasted Hummingbirds (1863-1864)
with Chromolithograph (1864)

The American painter Martin Johnson Heade

In both, they are Racquet-tailed Coquettes
arrayed above a nest, in which two eggs

barely crest the rim. The birds are green,
a white band, just above the tail.

The male shows his paddle feathers.
The female lifts her throat, aiming for the sky.

On canvas, we see a storm. The sky—
a scumbled greenish gray. There is light

only where the sun sets. In the hills
there is already rain. Consider his narrative—

Rain will fall. How gray clouds tell
a simple story dark. This was his plan for

the lithograph, too, but in the print, there is
no threat. Only a butter-yellow sky, dissolved

to an orange sunset. The birds seem joyous,
so happy in the print—

the male perky, the green understory, so spare.
No need for either to call across a distance.

There will never be a gulf, a distance,
between them. The artist cannot hand-

paint the storm onto every print.
It would break his heart to do this.

Strike the prints, then, and say *Forever.*
So many lies, the stones will not render them.

The Chambermaid's Story

The American painter Martin Johnson Heade,
16 Douro Place, Victoria Road, Kensington;
London, April 27, 1865

I come at ten to clean his room.
Mr. Heade is tired, he cannot leave his room.

Mr. Heade whispers; he says I'm not required.
I knock again upon his door. He will not leave his room.

He sends me off, then Stop! says he.
Will I buy the papers and bring them to his room?

I scurry to the corner—the April wind so cold.
Buy the Herald and the Times and bring them to his room.

I lay them at his door. *Lincoln Dead!* the headlines read.
Mr. Heade is sad, I hear weeping from his room.

I clean for Mr. Spencer, Mr. Davis, Mr. Smith.
Align the braided rug and stop again outside his room.

Mr. Heade's an artist who paints birds and jungle scenes.
I wonder at his genius, when'ere I clean his room.

Last night a ship from Boston brought word of Lincoln's death.
I heard the newsie's call in the street outside my room.

At tea, I offer biscuits when I knock upon his door
and leave a change of towels on the mat outside his room.

It may be that he is ill. I wait for near an hour.
Fetch a pail of coal and hear nothing from his room.

A dray clatters down the street. The gaslights are all lit.
I should stay no longer. There is silence in his room.

Silence. What am I to do? I am but Claire,
the chambermaid. Do I dare unlock his room?

Excerpt from an Unsent Letter
to Mrs. Laura Webb, Regarding
Ruby Throat of North America (1865)

The American painter Martin Johnson Heade,
in London, July 7, 1865

My project winds to a failed close.
The stones with which I proposed to lithograph
the brilliance of the hummers will not hold
the various inks—cannot fairly represent
the blues, the fire-struck greens, et cetera,
of the beauties I found during my stay in Brazil.
Each day I began in fresh hope, walking
the Thames toward the printers.
Each afternoon, atop the press or marking proofs,
I grew more despondent by the hour.
I returned at dusk to my studio in Kensington,
opened a claret and, working through the course
of a fortnight, painted a pair of Ruby Throats—
hummingbirds you would have known as a child.
The female, a delicate green, with pale underbelly,
perches within a blooming apple tree—
petals alive with pinks. The male, slightly elevated
to the right, watches; his throat, his thorax,
that wild rubious red, his back and and wings,
cadmium green, a color recalled in the leaves
of the tree, suggested again in the mix of blue
sky and the yellow-gold of clouds.
The hills are rounded—I mean them to speak
of Vermont or Maine—
of some New World, in any event.
The nest is empty and the bird's situation—

62

the green hills, the leaves of the apple tree,
the empty nest and pink blooms,
the near-buds—speak to some beginning.
Dare one say, a new love.

Across the great Atlantic, separated
as we are by your marriage, by convention
and the expectations of our times, made bold
by this wine, I have a confession.
During my stay at Petropolis, there,
at the summer house kept by your husband
in the mountains above Rio, you encouraged me
to visit without invitation, in the *primitavo*
way of that place. And so I would come
to your house unannounced, joining you
for breakfast, or for tea those languid afternoons.
One morning, I circled in the garden,
and found you without servants, bathing
in a pool formed by a mountain stream.
You did not hear me; of this I am certain.
Laura, I am a painter, and seeing your lovely form—
your dark hair let down, your breasts, your sex
as you left that pool; the music—of water as it spilled
over the slight dam of rocks, even, I imagined, of
your breathing—or was it the quiet hum of a song
as you dried yourself and reached for your robe?—
I did not look away. I have thought of this often;
am artist enough to contemplate the subject
fortune presented, gentleman enough to blush
as I write this, as the Ruby's throat blushes,
in the canvas I will post, before leaving this place.

Orpheus the Prophet

Salt washed, my right eye pecked sightless,
my left, still cloudy with sea water,
I loll about and say what they want to hear.
When fields are dry, I prophesy rain.
When asked for the stars, I say *Look at the sky.*
The blind shrimp that scurry, tap-tapping through the pools,
the cave bats that flap around and foul the stalagmites—
all of us are happy.

                    A swan, paddling the last round
of wintered water, foretells his own death,
singing more sweetly as it comes. Whenever
I must speak now, I speak in stagy whispers.
The vireo, the meadowlark, the tiniest sparrow—
name a songbird, nested among the darkening trees,
who will not prophesy the night.

Letter to Frederic Edwin Church at Olana

From the American painter Martin Johnson Heade,
at the 10th Street Studios, Manhattan,
November 30, 1865

Dear Frederick—

To sell a canvas of apple blossoms (pale, creamy pinks)
spreading from a vase, to sell one of my countless
marsh-and-river scenes (how many hayricks
are there in New Jersey?), these were my tasks.
Having accomplished them at the Union League's
November show—Christmas presents, no doubt, for
some ambitious lawyer's wife—I have two months' rent
and enclose it, with thanks for your patience
and the use of your workspace.

Kensett says a good Hello, also LaFarge. Bret Harte—
have you read his western stories?—asked of you.
Even old Bierstadt, in his brusque Teutonic yawp, asked
about your health (Beware!) and inquired specifically
of the little place you are building upriver.

I spend the days at my easel, though the winter light
begins to fail. I rarely go out, take no real
entertainment, though Gifford has a new model
in Studio 4. In late afternoons, it is not unknown
for her to trill away at his piano. Perhaps I will
wander over and join her in a song.

My best to Isabel, and to your young one, too.
Think of me, living this monastic life,
as you gaze upon the Hudson.

In two days time, perhaps three, what flotsam
touches your shore shall find its way
so very near my door.

Nocturne: From the 10th Street Studios to Fulton Street

From the notebooks of Martin Johnson Heade,
Manhattan, January 3, 1870

A daylong rain resolves in mist.
I go for dinner at eight—
a dozen oysters, bread, a Sauterne.
I cannot paint magnolias in darkness and cold.
After, I descend through the Bowery—
in the middle of life, pursued by beasts.
I pass bordellos, saloons, sipping brandy from a flask
I keep against my chest.
The gaslights are as flame-lit moons.
Mouths mutter, music startles
when doors open. A woman motions—
dressed in a shapeless cloak,
her hat plumed with sodden feathers.
Without hope in this circle, we live in desire.
Dark bodies gather at fires, tossing what
they muster—sticks, shattered packing crates—
onto the flames. I join a circle, nod, warm
my hands. A yardarm creaks
and from the starless sky, a splattering of fish!
The men wade among the carcasses,
throwing flounder, shoveling ice. Mid-harbor,
the Brooklyn Ferry plows home,
bearing the drowsy bodies of waitresses,
of coal-men and stevedores,
of the exhausted and the nearly dead.

Robert Mitchum Returns
to the Blue Haven Hotel

Mitchum retuned to reminisce a few years before his
death in 1997, but, upset at seeing the ruin, told his driver
to turn around and went straight back to the airport.
-Jim Clark, *The Daily Mail*, January 28, 2004

Mitchum lands in Tobago, says
"Blue Haven Hotel" and the driver looks confused.
"Out the road to Bacolet Point," Mitchum says,
making the driver stop at a tin-shack bodega
for rum and plastic cups.

Long-shot of a Cadillac, moving through the cane.
Mirror-shot—Mitchum lifts a cup to his lips.

The road is pot-holed, edged with glass shards
and hibiscus; the final hundred yards—Yes,
he remembers—the Royal Palms, those shabby old
sentinels, looming over the macadam.

He spies the pink shutters,
a few tossed chairs, can just see the edge
of the empty blue pool.

A green hummingbird—attending a magnolia
or guarding a nest—dives at his head.
Mitchum swats with the back of his hand—
the left that staggered Toxie Hall,
legendary sparring partner of Rocky Marciano.

Does he hear calypso music?
Mitchum forgets the broken bird,
the rolling azure sea.

Yes, he loved her here—
a flaming torch that marked
the tangled path to the deck, that starry night—
shot-reverse-shot—his hand pressed softly
along the small of her back.

End card—process shot of stars
cleaving against the sky.

Mitchum says "Let's go."
The petrels are screaming just beyond the point—
out where the bonefish cruise,
and waves slap time against the black
and barnacled rocks.

Tropical Landscape
with Ten Hummingbirds (1870)

> Received a letter from [Albert] Bierstadt last Thursday, who writes
> that cannot recommend me for the Astor commission, as "You are
> neither my colleague nor my student." How will I survive the
> coming winter? After two bitter days, I return to my tiny obsessions,
> sworn to array them across a larger canvas.
> -From the notebooks of Martin Johnson Heade,
> October 21, 1870

First—male Streamertail, upper left.
Iridescent green body and crested blue head,
your tail feathers cross in a blue X.
Jamaica-born, you look far beyond the canvas,
knowing you will never belong.
Only a strange wind could carry you
into these trees. What price, this small lie?
Your body pulled from a leather bag
and perched on a tendril of vine—
I return you to the dead,
buffered softly in cloth.

Next—Red-Tailed Comet,
upper center. Clutching at a bare stick,
you look across the lake, toward
the smoke of a distant gray volcano.
Long reddish tail,
black striped; your body
so oddly arched. You are cool-eyed—
yellow head aimed at a deadly fire.

Three—Horned Sun Gem,
center right. Green body, white shoulder,

black chest. Behind you, the trees bloom
in white, as if snowfall in Manhattan winter.
Atop your head, a crest; a small, birdbrained rainbow.
You are too happy here—your eye
quizzical, as though you grasp the fatal letter
in your black and tiny claw.

Crossing the wide canvas—ten passion flowers;
crimson. Nine closed and randomly arranged,
tangled among the three-lobed leaves.
One flower open, center right—ten petals
rolled back (said to represent Christ's faithful apostles—
the thread of purple around the style equaling the Crown
of Thorns, et cetera). Oh, Christian missionaries,
trying to explain God's lustful tropics!
To Darwin, the petals splay
to lure the hummers and for no other cause.

Fourth—Fork-Tailed Woodnymph,
frozen in flight. Creamy throat, blue
body in rain-blurred light.
Your tail rises forever—an elegant dark fin.
Something almost yields when the wings of birds
lock in mid-beat. *Lord, let the wind not fail us.*

Far right, two Tufted Coquettes.
The male spreads his wings before her green body,
as if forming a shield.
She is perched on a strand of vine,
facing left. Their bills almost touch.
For ten years, my beating wings, my heart-in-throat
warblings did not astound her.

Below, in near darkness,
hummingbirds seven and eight—
male and female Topaz.
Across his back, the flash of red, a crimson
that might be a coming bud.
His yellow head lifts; tail
slicing down across the canvas.
Behind him, she perches—
bronze, green throat,
staring into an open flower,
her torso, stilled in the tarnished light.
What can we know of her endless gaze
at desire—the bodies clasping
and the bodies letting go?

Ninth hummingbird, mid-canvas—
the Black-Eared Fairy, fluttering open, his body
a brilliant green, with black and emerald tail.
I say, *The green of envy*, and fluttering about
its empty air, bitterness—that small deadly bird,
resplendent—my last deadly sin.
If I fail my heart, it is because of you.

What remains? Tenth hummingbird—Ruby Topaz
on the lower left. Red head and white throat,
your body—jewel set in jeweled dark.
You point across the reedy lake,
keeping in view a mountain's distance.
And this is what I am left with—
a body singing, this midair pose
among three-lobed leaves. From this dark thicket
I begin again, sketching a flight to open water.

-for E.B.V.

Letter to Bridget Campbell
in Tobago

-Edward Campbell, Buffalo New York, April 24, 1946

Dearest—

Yesterday, I stopped in a small town in the Finger Lakes.
I stayed at an inn which featured roast duck—its skin
sizzling, crackled.

Across the road was an estate sale. A woman of Brazil-
ian descent was selling her grandmother's belongings—a
breakfront, canopied bed, china, etc. She said her grand-
mother was a *grande senhora* who had come to America in
the 1880's, after they deposed the last emperor of Brazil.

For three hundred dollars, I bought a painting of two hum-
mingbirds fighting beneath a pink orchid. The woman said
the artist was once a sweetheart of her grandmother, an
American, who'd gone to Brazil to paint hummingbirds.
The painting might work well above the check-in desk after
we've finished remodeling the hotel, or on that sea-foam
wall, guarding the entrance to the dining room.

Keep the plaster-men at work. I'll see the bankers, then fly
out on Wednesday. With connections in Miami and Kings-
ton, I should be home—hummingbirds humming—Friday
afternoon, latest.

Perhaps, love, before this note reaches your hand.

NOTES

The 1863-1864 journey of the American painter Martin Johnson Heade to Brazil is a matter of record, and I have looked to the work of Professor Theodore Stebbins, Jr.,* for certain details regarding that trip, Heade's work, and the artist's aesthetic approach to what he found in that country. Though reference is occasionally made in these poems to the notebooks of Martin Johnson Heade, I did not rely upon the actual notebooks (except for a few excerpts found in the work of Professor Stebbins) in composing the poems. While attentive to dates and certain facts, I have freely imagined Heade's personality, feelings, and response to historic events.

Martin Johnson Heade (1819-1905) is often grouped with the Hudson River School of American painters. Heade's close relationship with Frederic Edwin Church, and his friendships with Harriet Beecher Stowe, Professor Louis Agassiz, Ambassador and Mrs. James Watson (Laura) Webb, the Emperor Dom Pedro II, the Reverend James Cooley Fletcher and other figures represented in the text of these poems are known, though many of the specifics of these relationships have been fictionalized in this manuscript. Other figures—notably, Capitao Eduardo Gonzales, Rosa Gonzales (Anderson), Claire the Chambermaid, Nigel the Lithographer's Apprentice, the hoteliers Bridget and Edward Campbell, the Reverend and Mrs. Ian (Sarah) MacLeod—are imagined and did not necessarily exist.

The exact contents and order of appearance Heade intended for the *Gems of Brazil* series is unknown. Much of what experts believe was meant for inclusion in the bound volume of lithographs can be found in the Manoogian Collection, which is in private hands in Michigan.**

The painting *Tropical Landscape with Ten Hummingbirds* (1870) can be seen in the Seattle Museum of Art, on loan from the Roy Nutt Family Trust. *Approaching Thunderstorm* (1859) is in the permanent collection of the Metropolitan Museum of Art in New York. The painting *Sun Gems* (ca. 1864-1865), as recorded by Professor Stebbins, is lost, and is probably not decorating a hut in Brazil. The painting *Fighting Hummingbirds with Pink Orchid* (1875-1890) can be found in a private collection in Massachusetts, and has never been on display at the Blue Haven Hotel in Tobago. Sixteen of Heade's hummingbird paintings are in the permanent collection of the Crystal Bridge Museum of American Art in Bentonville, Arkansas. Other examples of Heade's work appear in museums and art collections across the United States and in Europe.

Several references are made in the poems to John Gould (1804-1881), an English ornithologist and illustrator who assisted Charles Darwin in the identification of various bird species. Gould published *A Monograph of the Trochilidae or Hummingbirds with 360 Plates* (1849-1861).

The German painter Albert Bierstadt (1830-1902) makes several appearances in these poems. Bierstadt is particularly known for his dramatic landscapes of the American west. The epigraph attributed to Bierstadt at p. 44, and the quotation attributed to him in the epigraph at p. 70, are fictional.

"A Vast Rosewood Aviary..." (p. 1). The Portuguese phrase "colibris, beija flor" means "hummingbirds, flower-kissers."

Letter to Harriet Beecher Stowe (pp. 2-4). Harriet Beecher Stowe (1811-1896) wrote the popular anti-slavery novel *Uncle Tom's Cabin* (1852). Her son, Frederick William Stowe (1840-?) was a captain in the Union Army when he suffered a severe head-wound at Cemetery Ridge on July 3, 1863, during the third day of the Battle of Gettysburg. Frederick never fully recovered from his injury and descended into alcoholism. During the summer of 1871, he disappeared near San Francisco, California.

"The price of wisdom is above rubies..." See: Proverbs 8:11; Job 28:18.

Flying Down to Rio (1933) (pp. 15-16). The film, directed by Thornton Wheeler, marked the first pairing of Ginger Rogers and Fred Astaire, albeit in secondary roles. The dancing-atop-the-wings sequence was an effort by RKO to compete with the extravagant Warner Brothers musicals choreographed by Busby Berkeley.

The inscriptions on the golden steps in *The Hummingbird Artist Dreams of the Ladder of Heaven* (pp. 17-18) are suggested by *The Ladder of Divine Ascent* (ca. 600 CE) a monastic treatise by St. John Climacus.

Fire Down Below (1957) (pp. 33-35). During filming, the cast stayed at the Blue Haven Hotel on Tobago, an island famous for its hummingbirds. *Fire Down Below* was the first film to feature Rita Hayworth following the dissolution of her tumultuous marriage to singer Dick Haymes. Immediately prior to Haymes, she had been married to Orson Welles. After the completion of filming, Robert Mitchum recorded an album of calypso songs, *Calypso is Like So* (1957).

The epigraph "What do you see?" attributed to Mark Rothko in *By Oil Lamp, The Hummingbird Artist Decants a Glass of Madeira and Contemplates Hooded Visorbearer* (1864-1865), (p. 36) is the opening line from *Red* (2010), John Logan's stage-play about Rothko.

Orfeu Negro (1959) (p. 37), a film directed by Marcel Camus, locates the story of Orpheus and Eurydice in a Rio de Janeiro *favela* during Carnival time.

It's All True (1942) (pp. 44-47). In 1942, while editing *The Magnificent Ambersons* (1942), Orson Welles was sent to Brazil by RKO Pictures and the United States government to make a film promoting cooperation between the United States and South America. Chaos ensued. The project envisioned by Welles far exceeded any available funding. Welles refused to report to the studio about his progress, and RKO eventually cancelled the project as it was being filmed. In 1993, *It's All True* was released as a documentary directed by Bill Krohn and Myron Meisel, assembling several portions of Welles' intended film.

One segment intended for the original film concerned the *Jangadeiros*, a group of fishermen from northern Brazil, making their way to Rio de Janeiro to petition the government for better wages and benefits. Jacare was the leader of the *Jangadeiros*. As Welles was filming the triumphal "arrival" of the fishermen in Rio harbor, Jacare's boat was capsized. When a rumor began that Jacare had been swallowed during an epic battle between a giant squid and a whale, Welles encouraged the story, since it exonerated his film crew from responsibility for Jacare's drowning.

Portions of Jacare's body were later found inside a shark.

The poet Alfonso Reyes was a Mexican diplomat stationed in Rio de Janeiro who befriended Welles during the filming of *It's All True*.

Letter to Professor Louis Agassiz, Posted with the Harbor Pilot, Rio de Janeiro (pp. 48-49). On April 5, 1864, the day after Martin Johnson Heade left for England, the naturalist Louis Agassiz of Harvard University arrived in Rio de Janeiro leading a scientific expedition the members of which included his wife, Elizabeth Cabot Cary Agassiz, and William James. Professor Agassiz had asked Heade to collect 100 hummingbird eggs for him in advance of the expedition. Among the American scientific community, Agassiz was the most well-known critic of Darwin's theory of natural selection. With his wife, Agassiz wrote *A Journey to Brazil* (1868).

Donald Duck in Brazil (pp. 50-51). In 1941, the United States government sent Walt Disney and a group of his studio artists to South America on a goodwill tour. The journey (with stops in Brazil, Argentina, Uruguay, and Peru) resulted in three animated films featuring Donald Duck: *Saludos Amigos* (1942), *The Three Caballeros* (1944) and

Clown of the Jungle (1947). The story of the South American journey is recounted in *Walt & El Grupo* (2008), a documentary film directed by Theodore Thomas.

In *Letter to Frederic Edwin Church at Olana* (pp. 69-70), the lines *The infernal serpent; he it was whose guile / stirred up with envy and revenge…* are from John Milton's *Paradise Lost*, Book I, lines 34-35.

Olana is the 250 acre estate on the Hudson River built by Frederic Edwin Church between 1860-1891. The site is now on the National Register of Historic Places and is operated as a public park by the State of New York. Heade often rented Church's space at the 10th Street Studios in Manhattan when Church was at Olana.

In *Nocturne: From the 10th Street Studios to Fulton Street* (p. 71) the line *Without hope in this circle, we live in desire…* is a slight variation on a line from *The Inferno* by Dante Alighieri, Circle 1, Canto 4:42.

---

* Theodore E. Stebbins, Jr., *Martin Johnson Heade* (Yale University Press, 1999); and *The Life and Work of Martin Johnson Heade: A Critical Analysis and Catalog Raisonné* (Yale University Press, 2000).

**Frances E. Smith, Editor, *American Painting from the Manoogian Collection* (National Gallery of Art, 1989)

ABOUT THE AUTHOR

GREG RAPPLEYE's poems have appeared in *Poetry, The Southern Review, Shenandoah, Virginia Quarterly Review, America,* and other literary journals, and have been widely anthologized. His second book of poems, *A Path Between Houses* (University of Wisconsin Press, 2000) won the Brittingham Prize in Poetry. His third book, *Figured Dark* (University of Arkansas Press, 2007), was first runner-up for the Dorset Prize and was published in the Miller Williams Poetry Series. His numerous awards include the *Arts & Letters Prize* for poems appearing in this volume, the 49th Parallel Award from *Bellingham Review,* the *Mississippi Review* Prize in Poetry, the *Greensboro Review* Prize, The Paumanok Poetry Award, and a Pushcart Prize. A former Bread Loaf Fellow, he is a graduate of the University of Michigan Law School and the MFA Program for Writers at Warren Wilson College. He lives in an old blueberry house just north of the Grand River in Ottawa County, Michigan, with his wife Marcia, their two younger sons and three dogs. Retired now from the active practice of law, he teaches in the English Department at Hope College in Holland, Michigan.